Active
Archaeology
NOTEBOOK

First published in 2018 in paperback in the United States of America
by Thames & Hudson Inc., 500 Fifth Avenue, New York, New York 10110

thamesandhudsonusa.com

Library of Congress Control Number: 2018950319

ISBN 978-0-500-84113-6

Printed and bound in China by C & C Offset Printing Co. Ltd

Table of Contents

Preface

As a science and social study, archaeology is an active discipline. Archaeologists gather data to answer questions about the human past. Archaeology requires fieldwork, analysis, and collaborative research to develop accurate insights and new questions.

Learning about archaeology in a classroom often means that you do not get a good sense of how active archaeology really is. Professors are hindered by walls, desks, and time constraints. This workbook changes all of that! Through these activities, your instructor will help you to investigate like an archaeologist, get active and learn what it means to DO archaeology!

Introduction to Archaeology

1. Questions First
Leah McCurdy

Every scientific endeavor starts with a question. All questions that archaeologists investigate relate to big questions about the human past, such as "How did people organize themselves in society?" or "How did people get food and what did they eat?"

It is essential that archaeologists focus their research because archaeology works on the basis of the scientific method and the philosophy of science that underpins that method. To develop knowledge or understand something about the world (past, present, or future), scientists develop hypotheses or predictions based on their questions. These hypotheses must be "testable." This means that there must be some way to collect information that can lead to assessing whether the hypothesis or prediction is valid.

Focused case study questions, e.g. "Why did the classic period Maya culture build such large monuments, such as the pyramidal temples of Tikal?", can be addressed because archaeologists are able to visit a place like Tikal, survey or excavate the temples, and analyze how they were built and what they contain. Many other cultures around the world also built monumental temples. Correlating all those case studies can lead to understanding another big question: "Why do humans build large structures?"

For this activity, think of a specific time and place that interests you. Imagine you are an archaeologist starting a new research project. You will develop a testable archaeological research question focused on a case study of interest. You will share this question with your instructor and the class. After hearing all the questions developed by your classmates, think about what they have in common and what this suggests are the most important types of questions.

1 Use the map above to mark a location in the world that interests you. Have you already studied a place that you found interesting? Is there a place you really want to visit?

2 Near the location you marked, indicate a time period that is most interesting to you. The reign of one ruler? The earliest occupation of that place? A conquering event? Do you want to investigate a culture that lived 12,000 years ago or a group of people that lived 120 years ago?

3 Based on your interests documented on the map, develop a case study research question that relates in some way to one of the big questions of archaeology. Use this example as a guide: "Why did the classic period Maya culture build such large monuments, such as the pyramidal temples of Tikal?" As you are developing your question, consider the following:

- Do you state the case (time and place) in your question?

- Have you identified a specific group of people or culture? If so, include them in the question. If unknown, your question can include trying to figure out who they are.

- Is it too big? Is it specific enough that it is testable? Could you go out to that place and investigate in order to find answers to this question?

4 Write your question here:

5 As you are listening to the questions designed by other students, take notes on any commonalities and patterns that you recognize in the nature of the questions and shared interests.

2. 3D Tours
Leah McCurdy

This is a class activity that requires access to an internet-enabled computer or smartphone for a 3D experience.

3D video and virtual reality (VR) were once science fiction dreams. Today, 3D movies and VR technologies such as Oculus Rift and Google Cardboard have made this dream accessible to the public and to you as a student. VR technology is now integrated into mapping applications, such as Google Street View, so that you can visit distant places wherever you are.

Archaeologists have been working with virtual technologies for decades, incorporating them into research projects and/or using them to make images, videos, and games for the public. Archaeologists create virtual reconstructions of ancient structures based on their survey and excavation findings. They also use satellite data and photographic techniques to compile images and make whole virtual landscapes of the past. With the use of VR headsets and freely available applications, soon archaeologists will be able to share their findings and reconstructions with large audiences around the world.

In this activity, you will experience a famous archaeological site in 3D and/or virtual reality using freely available online resources. Take a tour of amazing archaeological sites in your classroom!

For a VR experience, you can use an internet-enabled smartphone (iOS or Android) with the Google Street View app downloaded and a VR headset such as Google Cardboard, which can be created by hand using free templates and tutorials available online. The app specific to the VR headset must also be downloaded to the smartphone prior to this activity.

1 Use Google Maps (http://maps.google.com) to navigate to Egypt. Navigate to Giza (Nazlet El-Semman, Al Haram, Egypt). In the bottom right-hand corner of the screen, click on the orange standing figure to see the "Street View" options. Choose the blue line that runs through the Giza Necropolis to be able to walk around the site.

2 As you are viewing Giza, respond to the following:

  a Describe the remains that you see, using terms relevant to the archaeological record.

  b Do you see evidence of formation processes? How so?

3 Using the recommendations below, visit at least one other archaeological site.

  a Tikal, Guatemala (Search "Tikal." Find "Acrópolis Norte.")
  b Taj Mahal, Agra, India. (Search "Taj Mahal, Agra.")
  c Baths of Caracalla, Rome, Italy. (Search "Baths of Caracalla.")
  d Angkor Wat Temple, Cambodia. (Search "Angkor Wat.")
  e Parthenon, Acropolis of Athens, Greece. (Search "Parthenon.")

4 As you are viewing your second site from the list above, describe one feature that it has in common with the Giza complex.

Material Evidence

3. Garbology
Crystal A. Dozier

Garbology is the study of garbage, or refuse, to help us understand human decisions and behaviors. In archaeology, 90 percent of the work is exactly that: looking through the trash and broken artifacts that people have left behind. Archaeologists call these trash deposits middens and analyze the assemblages within them to understand past behavior. These middens may include the refuse of one person or an entire village, from a single event or an extended period of years or decades.

Within trash accumulations, different materials give different insights into different aspects of human decisions and behaviors. But not all materials survive within the archaeological record. Unless preserved by extreme cold, extreme aridity, lack of oxygen, or burning, most organic material (things made of living things, such as wood or food) will decay. In this activity, you will explore how archaeologists reconstruct past behavior from garbage and theorize about what kind of generalizations or obstacles archaeologists encounter.

For the next three days, conduct garbology data collection of your own trash. Use the worksheet (on p. 13) to keep a log of everything you throw away in your bedroom or bathroom trash. Choose only one trashcan. At the same time each day, take note of the contents using the worksheet.

- For the "Item" column, briefly name the item you throw away, so that you can remember it for later reflection (i.e. be more specific than "food wrapper" by writing, for example, "CLIF Bar wrapper.")

- For the "Biodegradable" column, indicate Y for yes or N for no.

- Count the number of the same item and note the number in that column.

- In the "Indications of date?" column, note any chronological information that one could derive from observing this piece of trash. Imagine that someone a hundred years in the future finds your trash and is trying to figure out when it was made, used, or deposited.

- For the "Artifact class" column, use the following possibilities: Food Waste; Hygiene; Work/School; Entertainment/Recreation; Other.

1 What is the most common artifact class found in your garbage?

2 What does a high frequency of that artifact class imply about your behavior?

3 What in your garbage would survive 1,000 years of organic decay?

4 If that was the only thing to survive from your whole assemblage of trash, what might a future archaeologist infer about your behavior (without knowledge of any of the other items)?

5 What behaviors, habits, and experiences in your life might future archaeologists miss if this was the only assemblage from which they were inferring about your life?

Item	Bio-degradable?	Count	Indications of date?	Artifact class

Survey

4. On-the-ground

Joshua J. Lynch

Archaeological field methods can be divided into two major phases: survey and excavation. Survey allows archaeologists to identify archaeological materials and their distribution across a landscape, while excavations facilitate in-depth studies of individual places, identified through survey. Survey methodologies break down into three major categories; systematic, randomized, and high-probability locality surveys.

In this activity you will establish a survey methodology and apply your methodology to a fictional landscape. Archaeological sites, features, and structures present on the landscape will be revealed to you based on the survey methodology that you choose. You will use the results of your survey to provide an interpretation of site distribution, resource exploitation, and occupational history of the fictional landscape. Finally, you will be asked to provide plans for future survey, excavation, and preservation efforts based on your preliminary survey results.

You are managing an archaeological survey crew tasked with determining which type of archaeological remains survive in this landscape. Find the map of the area you need to survey. Inspect its features and their size. Use the worksheet to choose a survey methodology and get to work surveying the area. The maximum number of parcel squares you can investigate based on your funding is twenty.

This is the landscape you will survey (you will need to rotate the notebook to see the map clearly). Inspect the major geographic features and locations. The grid divides the survey area into square parcels labeled A1, A2, etc.

1 Select one of the survey methodologies described below to investigate the archaeological materials (historic and prehistoric) surviving in this landscape. Circle which survey methodology you choose from the list below and write two to three sentences explaining your choice.

Systematic surveys utilize an arbitrary pattern of survey applied uniformly across the landscape. This methodology is designed to minimize survey bias by archaeologists, but risks ignoring high-potential localities.

To conduct a **systematic survey**, choose twenty square parcels that create a uniform pattern across the area. Checkerboard patterns are very common. On the map, shade or outline the parcels you will survey.

Randomized surveys attempt to eliminate any sort of bias of the researchers. This methodology uses random numbers or choices to choose survey locations. It is very rarely encountered in the real world of archaeological field projects.

To conduct a **randomized survey**, pull twenty numbers and letters out of a hat to select square parcels or find a random number generator online. On the map, shade or outline the parcels you will survey.

High-probability locality surveys allow archaeologists to choose survey parcels that they judge as having a high probability of yielding archaeological materials. This survey method allows archaeologists to apply knowledge of landscape use, settlement patterns, and site distribution to inform selection. It is the most prone to the influence of the survey bias of the researchers.

To conduct a **high-probability locality survey**, choose the twenty square parcels that you think are most likely to contain archaeological remains. On the map, shade or outline the parcels you will survey.

2 Based on your methodology selection, your crew has surveyed the area and recorded their findings on the **Survey Results Table (supplied by your instructor)**. In the log below, document the findings within the square parcels included in your survey only. You will use these findings to develop interpretations.

SURVEY RESULTS LOG		
	Square parcel grid label	**Findings**
1		
2		
3		
4		
5		
6		
7		
8		
9		
10		
11		
12		
13		
14		
15		
16		
17		
18		
19		
20		

3 In the space below, write a short response reporting the results of your survey. What types of remains did you find? What do they reveal about landscape use practices, resource exploitation, site distribution, and the occupational history of this landscape? Do these patterns change through time?

4 Using your interpretations of the survey data, what would your next steps in assessing this landscape be? Provide a short plan for future survey, excavation, and preservation in this area.

5 Look at all the data on the **Survey Results Table**. How does total knowledge of the archaeological materials on the landscape change your interpretation? Do you feel like your survey methodologies helped you to create an accurate understanding of the archaeology of this area?

5. Submerged

Morgan F. Smith

Thanks to my father, for inspiring the idea

This is a class activity that requires PowerPoint slides.

Conducting science in different physical environments can be difficult. Some of the most difficult environments to investigate on Earth are not on land, but are underwater. Safety, time management, and immediate preservation are just some of the major considerations that underwater archaeologists need to keep in mind while conducting investigations. Submerged sites in lakes and off coastlines are investigated by archaeologists in different ways than those on land because of the particular challenges that underwater environments present.

Underwater archaeologists often have to work in water where visibility is less than 1 meter (approx. 3 feet). Even when water is clear, underwater excavations disturb bottom sediments and can quickly reduce visibility to zero. This is akin to doing archaeology in the dark. Furthermore, performing archaeology underwater is difficult due to the tendency of excavation materials to float away or become lost. Also, communication is limited to hand signals or writing underwater. Due to these constraints, pre-dive planning is imperative. This requires you to know your colleagues and work as a team. This activity will give you a glimpse into what underwater archaeology is like. Try your hand at mapping artifacts in conditions meant to mimic an underwater excavation! Make sure you hold onto that pencil!

Find a partner. You are working on a remarkable prehistoric archaeological site in North America, now underwater due to the rise in sea level at the end of the last Ice Age. You estimate that the site is about 13,000 years old. Use the worksheet to document the site as best you can in underwater conditions.

1 **Before you submerge**. Collaborate with your partner to design a research plan. Keep in mind that you will have only five minutes of oxygen! What do you want to record about artifacts or site features? What will be the most important information to document in the time you have? Remember that creating an accurate map of the site is critical to prove the significance of the site to your colleagues.

In the space below, write at least three types of information you will collect.

a _____

b _____

c _____

2 **You are now submerged!** You have geared up and are diving down to the submerged site. You can no longer talk to your partner as you would on land. To communicate, write notes on a sheet of paper or use hand signals. As diving requires you to have a regulator in your mouth at all times, you cannot mouth words.

3 When the site becomes visible, you and your partner have five minutes to record all data possible. Use the space below to take notes, sketch, etc. **Beware of underwater challenges that might arrive while you work!**

Dating

6. Human Time
Crystal A. Dozier

The study of *Homo sapiens* is not limited to anthropology and archaeology, but archaeology is the only methodology that allows us to understand the vast history of our species. As you will explore, the advent of writing occurred relatively late in human history. The study of human history using just written records is biased toward those who could write and what writings survive. Archaeology provides an independent methodology to study the past and humanity's history.

There are three main timescales used to date events or periods. Archaeologists use all three timescales, depending on the context of what they are researching. Those who study the past need to be able to switch between timescales:

- BP (before present). This scale was developed primarily to tell time in the distant past, in coordination with radiocarbon dating. Radiocarbon dating relies on the ratio of different isotopes of carbon within the atmosphere and the regular decay of the isotope ^{14}C. Atomic-bomb testing in the mid-twentieth century drastically altered the ratio of different carbon isotopes within the atmosphere, so the year zero BP is equivalent to the year 1950 AD/CE. BP counts backward, so the year 1 BP is equivalent to 1949 AD/CE.

- BC/AD (before Christ, anno Domini). This scale is the most commonly used timeline today. AD refers to anno Domini (Latin for "year of the Lord") which denotes time after the birth of Jesus of Nazareth, the most important figure to Christians. BC refers to "before Christ." This timescale was not used until the spread of Christianity through Europe. It became the predominant timescale only after European colonization across many regions.

- BCE/CE (before Common Era, Common Era). This scale uses the same timescale and same zero point as BC/AD, but uses a more generalized terminology, especially to talk about regions of the world where Christianity is not the major religious tradition.

Event	BP	BC/AD	BCE/CE	Relative date
Humans reach Australia				
Wheat first domesticated				
Humans reach North America				
Dogs first domesticated				
Great Pyramid at Giza built				
Stonehenge built				
Sumerian cuneiform invented				
Columbus arrives in the New World				
United States Declaration of Independence signed				
Start of the Common Era				
Qin era Great Wall of China				
Ming era Great Wall of China				
Radiocarbon dating "zero"				
Humans reach Europe				
Anatomically modern *Homo sapiens* in Africa				

In this activity, investigate important events in human history by determining their chronology relative to other events. Translate this chronology to multiple timescales. Using your textbook and other reliable resources, find dates for the major events in human history included on the worksheet. Based on the information you gather, translate dates into the BP, BC/AD, and BCE/CE scales. Using the far right column, put the events in relative order, from earliest (1) to latest (15).

Visual Timeline

Using the table of events, create a visual timeline scaled accurately so you can visualize how distant certain events are from each other:

- Using notebook paper or another material, create the base of your visual timeline. This can be a football field if you want! Or make it out of Lego!

- Select the scale. If you are using notebook paper, something like 1 cm = 2,000 years would make your timeline about four sheets long in landscape.

- Based on the events and their dates, mark the approximate center of your timeline with the appropriate date and event.

- Add events on either side of the center according to the chronology and scale by writing or inserting markers with labels. Can you find fifteen friends to mark events on your football-field timeline?

- If you chose something like a football field as your base "material," document your timeline as best you can with a photograph.

Reflection

1 Explain how relative and absolute timescales are different.

2 What scale did you use within your timeline (for example, how many centimeters/ Lego pieces/whatever to a year)? Did you encounter any difficulties creating your timeline to scale?

3 For how much of human history does writing not appear, before Sumerian cuneiform? Relate your answer as a percentage of time from the emergence of *Homo sapiens*. This is the amount of time in which archaeology is the only way to study humans.

4 In what situations might using BP be a more appropriate timescale? When would BCE/CE be most appropriate? When would BC/AD be most appropriate?

Classification

7. Store Typology

Leah McCurdy

This activity is based on an idea by Dr. Robin Robertson

Typology in archaeology uses the old saying "like goes with like" to categorize artifacts collected during surface collections, survey, or excavations. This categorization, or "typing," helps investigators find patterns in how artifacts were made, used, or discarded in the past. These patterns often help us date artifacts (using such techniques as seriation) and learn more about the people who made and used them.

In this activity, you will create your own typology of objects, or "finds," from a store of your choice. This typology will help you analyze an "assemblage of finds" and practice a fundamental step in artifact analysis. Such analyses can be used to consider artistic trends and techniques; technologies; social systems; occupational specialization; and economic relationships.

Visit a nearby store. *No purchase necessary! You do not need to buy any of your "finds."* Choose a type of object (or artifact) of which you can find ten different examples (e.g. ten different porcelain plates with different decoration or shapes). Once you have your finds, create your typology using the worksheet.

1 What store did you visit?

2 What object (artifact) did you choose?

3 Observe each find for similarities or differences in three different attributes. Some attributes you might focus on can include **color, size, shape, texture, pattern,** or **content**. Use the table below to document each of your finds. Choose the attributes that are the most relevant to you and write them in the first row of the table (the blanks labeled Attributes 1–3). Using the columns beneath, document these attributes for each of your finds.

	Attribute 1:	Attribute 2:	Attribute 3:
Find 1			
Find 2			
Find 3			
Find 4			
Find 5			
Find 6			
Find 7			
Find 8			
Find 9			
Find 10			

MY TYPOLOGY:		Find numbers – there will be multiple
Type 1 name		
Type 2 name		
Type 3 name		
Type 4 name		
Type 5 name		
Type 6 name		
Type 7 name		

4 Categorize your finds into *types* in the table above (or categories of your typology) based on their similarities. Everyone will have a different number of groups or types because all assemblages will be different. *You may have as few as three or as many as seven types.*

5 Use the table above to develop your typology. Determine how many types your assemblage requires (based on the distribution of similarities and differences). Name your types (based on the most relevant attributes; e.g. "Red Spotted"). Document which finds (by their number) you categorize within each type. Give your typology a title at the top of the table.

6 Which attribute within your assemblage was the most important in your typology (i.e. what attribute did you pay the most attention to while forming these types)? Use the categories of artifact analysis as a guide to address this question.

Social Organization

8. Campus Complexity

Rebecca Friedel
This activity was adapted from an idea by Leah McCurdy

Archaeologists study social complexity to understand the differences between and changes within societies across space and time. Identifying social complexity involves taking into account many factors. In archaeology, these factors manifest themselves in certain material remains within the archaeological record. Just like any material remains, remains of complexity are subject to formation processes, making some factors easier to identify than others. The material remains of complexity help us to determine the degree to which societies are structured and how inequalities played a role in these structures.

Such state-level societies as ours are on the high end of the complexity spectrum. They exhibit many factors of complexity including:

1 **Large population** wherein many people co-exist and interact frequently.

2 Inequality among segments of the population; and **social stratification**.

3 **Economic specialization** and subsistence dependence on others with "**delayed return**."

4 Regulation through customs and **laws** to govern behavior, interactions, and exchange.

5 **Hierarchical ruling** structure for administration and maintenance of order.

6 **Agricultural intensification** to provide surplus to support non-food-producing groups.

7 Interactions beyond the local community including **trade and exchange**.

8 **Institutionalized ideology**, rituals, and artistic expression representing the community.

9 **Prominent monuments** representing the community and/or those in power.

In this activity, you will identify factors of social complexity as seen on your own campus. These factors can be found in many places on campus and may leave different material remains, depending on the activities associated with each factor.

Visit campus and plan enough time to walk around all the primary areas. Don't forget paper, a pencil, and a clipboard (or something hard to write on) while "in the field."

1 Using the table below, document *at least five* different factors of complexity, where you identified them, and how they would show up in the archaeological record (taking into account formation processes). Think like an archaeologist as you walk around the campus. Does the campus exhibit complexity? How would archaeologists be able to recognize these factors? Identify *at least five factors*.

Factor from activity description	Where is the factor represented on campus?	What are its physical / material attributes?	List one formation process that could affect this material

2 Imagine you are an archaeologist who just discovered the ancient site of this campus 1,000 years from now. Imagine you discover the remains of *two of the factors of complexity* you identified above. What would they look like 1,000 years from now? Sketch a plan or bird's-eye view of the "remains" of two factors on separate sheets of paper. Label them appropriately. Try to keep it to scale and don't forget to include titles!

Geoarchaeology

9. pHreservation

Morgan F. Smith and Leah McCurdy
Thanks to the USDA for creating the open access Web Soil Survey

This activity requires a computer with internet accessibility.
Geoarchaeologists specialize in the application of techniques from the geosciences to archaeological sites or assemblages. The bread and butter of geoarchaeology is understanding soils and sediments. The properties of soils and sediments affect what survives over long periods of time. Certain soil and sediment conditions are more likely to preserve certain types of artifacts and organic materials. One important condition to consider is pH, or the measure of a soil's acidity or basicity (how alkaline/basic it is). The table below indicates how pH is measured (in terms of numerical value) and how conditions relate to preservation.

Prior to surveying for archaeological sites in a given geographic area, a cursory survey of soils in the region can increase efficiency and accuracy of work. Considering the properties of soils and sediments can help archaeologists to develop predictions about conditions and to be better prepared for specific findings. This activity will walk you through how to use the Web Soil Survey tool provided by the US Department of Agriculture. You will use this tool to understand more about soils and sediments in an area of your own choosing, and explore how soil data is helpful for archaeological interpretations.

pH level	Condition	Preservation potential for artifacts	Preservation potential for organics
Less than 6.5	Acidic	ceramics; wood	pollen; seeds; charred remains; phytoliths; soil diatoms; skin
6.5–7.5	Neutral	ceramics; wood; textiles; iron; copper; glass; plaster and mortar	bone; seeds; charred remains; phytoliths; soil diatoms; molluscs (>7)
Greater than 7.5	Alkaline	ceramics; wood; textiles (7.5–8); iron; copper; glass; plaster and mortar	bone; molluscs; phytoliths

Table based on information provided by SASSA: Soil Analysis Support System for Archaeology

Follow the guides and questions in the worksheet to locate data that will help you to evaluate the pH preservation potential of an area that interests you archaeologically.

1 Find the US Web Soil Survey at the weblink below. Click the large green button labeled "Start WSS." https://websoilsurvey.sc.egov.usda.gov/App/HomePage.htm

2 Once the WSS populates, you will see a map of the continental United States. Use the toolbar above the map to zoom in (magnifying glass) and pan around (hand tool) to find an area of interest. Ensure that you zoom in quite far, because the Web Soil Survey *will not* allow you to select an area greater than 100,000 acres.

3 Once you have zoomed in, click the rectangle "AOI" (area of interest) button and select an area. It is fine if your selected AOI includes more than one soil survey.

4 In the space below, briefly describe the location of your AOI. Provide latitude and longitude for precise location.

5 After selecting an AOI, you will be directed to a new page with several tabs.

- The "Soil Map" tab details "units" of soil and sediment distributed within the AOI.

- The "Soil Data Explorer" offers new tabs, including "Soil Properties and Qualities."

- On the left, "Properties & Qualities Ratings" includes "Soil Chemical Properties."

- Choose the "pH" section and complete the following tasks.

6 Select the "Surface Layer" button and click "View Rating." In the space below, sketch the *surface layer pH map* of your AOI with all unit areas. Using the pH table, label the pH rating of each unit.

7 Select the "Depth Range" button. Enter a top depth of 50 cm and bottom depth of 60 cm. Click "View Rating." In the space below, sketch the 50–60-cm *depth pH map* of your AOI. Label the pH rating of each unit.

8 Enter a top depth of 100 cm and bottom depth of 110 cm. Click "View Rating." Sketch the 100–110-cm *depth pH map* of your AOI below. Label the pH rating of each unit.

9 Enter a top depth of 200 cm and bottom depth of 210 cm. Click "View Rating." In the space below, sketch the 200–210-cm *depth pH map* of your AOI. Label the pH rating of each unit.

10 Using what you know about the potential for preservation in different soil conditions (refer to the pH table), what types of artifacts and organic remains would you expect to find in each level of your AOI? Create a *depth* diagram or simple *stratigraphic* diagram that illustrates this information below.

Environmental Archaeology

10. EcoClues
Leah McCurdy

This is a class activity for which cards will be handed out by the instructor.
Archaeology is all about context: the context of artifacts and finds in the archae-ological record and reconstructing the context of ancient groups. One of the primary components of an ancient group's context is its environment. Where did the group members live? Was it hot? Was it cold? Did they have access to fresh water sources? What sort of animals could they hunt? In addition to providing details of environmental context, answering these questions leads to reconstructing subsistence practices.

Subsistence practices are the means by which people maintain themselves and their social group. This primarily relates to getting/storing/making food and water. Subsistence practices can also relate to shelter and other aspects of landscape use.

Archaeologists are interested in reconstructing environmental contexts over time and how humans modified their environments to suit their needs. Collecting evidence for such questions often leads to inferences and interpretations regarding subsistence practices and how they change over time.

You recently made an important discovery that can help us to reconstruct subsistence practices within a specific environmental context. Describe and analyze your find. Then, collaborate with a research team to compile all the evidence from your context. With the complete dataset, make informed reconstructions of subsistence practices in this environment and consider whether/how they changed over time.

1. Analyze your find.

Your find (describe briefly)	
What type of find is it (circle one)?	ARTIFACT ECOFACT FEATURE
Explain why your find is an artifact, ecofact, or feature. Was it recovered from a different type of find?	What subcategories are relevant to these finds? What kind of artifact, ecofact, or feature are they?

2. Locate colleagues that have discovered finds in the same context as you.

Briefly describe the context of your find.	
Which environmental setting does your context relate to most?	TROPICAL ARID WATERLOGGED COLD
Describe the preservation expectations in this environment.	

3. Record all lines of evidence (finds) discovered by the research team investigating within your context.	What is the significance of each line of evidence?

4. What inferences can your research team make about subsistence practices from this collection of evidence? What change occurred according to the evidence? What is unique about this context? Your team will present these findings and inferences to the class.

Experimental Archaeology

11. *Atlatl* Games
Leah McCurdy

Humans have always been interested in improving their technology. From the first stone-tool production by flint knapping, creators innovated new techniques. One important innovation that was developed by different groups in different places around the world is known today as the *atlatl*. This is the name given to the spear-thrower apparatus in the Nahua language of the Aztec culture. *Atlatls* are carved with a spur that allows for the end of a dart (or spear) to be secured at one end and held with the hand at the other end. The thrower propels the spear by swinging the *atlatl* forward. With this method, spears reach higher speeds and travel longer distances.

Atlatls were used as early as the Upper Paleolithic, often carved from animal bone, ivory, or wood. The Aztec and other Mesoamerican groups used the *atlatl* to hunt mammals and to fish. Ancient and modern Inuit of the Canadian and Alaskan Arctic use the spear-thrower to hunt such marine animals as walrus and even whale. Australian Aborigines call their spear-throwers *woomeras* and used them alongside spears and boomerangs to hunt.

In this activity, you will get the opportunity to use an *atlatl* for yourself. Along with your classmates, you will conduct experimental archaeology to understand better the benefits of the *atlatl*. You will collect and analyze data to test a hypothesis.

You will conduct experimental archaeological data collection to answer the following research question:

Does arm length correlate to the achievement of greater distance when throwing with an *atlatl*?

1 Data Collection – Instructions

- Divide into teams of two.

- Each student will be able to practice throwing the *atlatl* before any distances are recorded.

- While waiting to take your practice throws, measure and record the physical attributes in the data-collection table with the help of your teammate.

- Each student will conduct measured throws and record both distances and accuracy.

- To ensure that no data is lost, find another team and share your datasets. Record the team's data in your data-collection table.

Your team							
Thrower	Arm length	Total height	Stride length	First trial distance	First trial accuracy (good, fair, or poor)	Second trial distance	Second trial accuracy (good, fair, or poor)

Another team							
Thrower	Arm length	Total height	Stride length	First trial distance	First trial accuracy (good, fair, or poor)	Second trial distance	Second trial accuracy (good, fair, or poor)

2 Respond to the following questions as you are waiting to complete your throwing trials:

a By conducting this experiment, what can we learn about people who used the *atlatl* as a subsistence technology?

b Consider whether there are any flaws in the way data was collected in this experiment. Does your team foresee any issues with this dataset? Consider how we could improve upon this experiment based on your concerns.

c Despite these concerns, does the data collected by your team and the other team you collaborated with support the original research question?

d Construct a different research question that can be addressed by the data you are being asked to collect. If you want to consider a research question that would require additional data, make sure you note what other data you would need to collect.

Bioarchaeology

12. Guess Who's Dead!
Leah McCurdy and Emily A. Sharp

This is a class activity that requires PowerPoint slides.

Bioarchaeologists are tasked with reconstructing the life histories of individuals that died long ago. By closely examining an individual's skeleton and teeth, researchers can estimate such attributes as how long a person lived, what they ate, and where they grew up. Burial context also plays a vital role in our interpretations of ancient lifeways.

In this activity, you will work with a classmate on a bioarchaeology project. You are tasked with figuring out the identity of each person described in eleven case studies. You will piece together multiple lines of evidence to make a positive identification. Think back to the board game *Guess Who?* to get into the spirit!

Pair up into teams of two. You will be presented with eleven case studies of human remains or ancient burials. You must pay close attention to all the evidence provided to deduce which of the identities in the options table best fits with that evidence. In other words, GUESS WHO'S DEAD!

When you think you have identified the individual correctly, one of the teammates should raise a hand. Correct identifications earn your team a point. Teams will compete to see who identifies the most case studies correctly.

Guess Who's Dead! options table – use these options to guess the identity of the dead person.

Adult female archaeologist murdered by looters	Alien that died on earth due to alien–human conflict	Adult male priest buried with vestments and altar objects	Sub-adult male orphan killed in a church
Sub-adult female who suffered from anemia and may have been considered possessed	High-status adult male craft specialist interred with prized creations	Person who drowned as the result of a shipwreck during a long-distance journey	Sixty-year-old female craft specialist who suffered from arthritis
Adult male killed via boomerang and interred in an above-ground method	Child from an ancient cultural group with modern living descendants	High-status adult female who died after falling from a horse	Adult female slave sacrificed as part of the burial goods for a master's grave
Adult male shaman who suffered from malnutrition early in life	Adult male who participated in routine stressful and dangerous physical activity	Adult male whose primary subsistence was focused on marine resources	Child from a mobile society who grew up in one place, moved around, and returned to the birthplace
High-status female child buried with a prized domesticated animal	Adult male who died of natural causes while many of his generation died in physical conflict	Thirty-year-old person who ate a good balance of nutrient-rich plants and animal protein	High-status adult male with great expectations for the afterlife
Child who suffered from malnutrition	Sub-adult female without any signs of ill-health; may have been sacrificed	Male child who suffered from severe malnutrition and likely died of starvation	Adult male who was murdered due to suspicions of vampirism

13. Head Aches

Emily A. Sharp

Head injuries are one of the most important lines of evidence in investigations of past violence and warfare. Bioarchaeologists analyze human remains for evidence of skeletal trauma—a proxy for violence—and compare rates of injury across populations. To estimate the frequency of violence in a population, researchers count the number of people affected with trauma and compare it to the total number of individuals.

In large, comparative data surveys, archaeologists often evaluate the presence or absence of a certain variable across broad timescales and geographic coverage. Archaeologists must consider issues related to sample selection bias when analyzing these patterns. In this activity, you will gain a better understanding of how archaeologists analyze data to make inferences about certain behaviors through a bioarchaeological case study.

You are starting a research project, and you want to know how rates of violence have changed through time. You decide to focus your data analysis on skeletal trauma and on collections that date to before the rise of states. After a preliminary literature search, you find thirteen sites where human skeletal remains have been excavated and where you can get permission to analyze the remains for evidence of injuries. These sites span a time range of over 15,000 years and are located across the world.

1 Using the space below, construct a hypothesis that tests how, or even if, you think violence changed over time (consider whether you think violence increased, decreased, or remained constant over time). Your hypothesis should be a statement of your expectation.

You have finished collecting the data and now want to visualize how many people were affected with trauma at the different sites by creating the bar chart below. You decide to show the data as a percentage (x-axis). Sites are listed as A-M and time periods are in parentheses (y-axis), arranged in order of date.

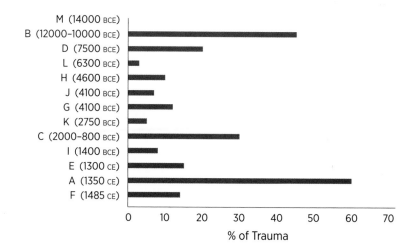

2 Based on this graph, can you draw any conclusions regarding how rates of trauma changed through time? If you can, what are those conclusions? If you cannot, why not?

3 Do you think the dataset is a representative sample (a small quantity that actually reflects the larger whole it represents) to examine change through time across 15,000 years? Why or why not? Consider what is missing.

You now want to gain a better understanding of site context and circumstances surrounding how the individuals you examined received traumatic injuries. Based on previous archaeological studies, you know that all the individuals you examined from Site A died around the same time. Archaeologists believe they were massacred during a raid on a prehistoric village in what is now South Dakota in the United States. In contrast, individuals from Site B died at various times throughout a 2,000-year time span in ancient Nubia, Africa. Some likely died violent deaths during large-scale war, while others may have incurred injuries during smaller, interpersonal conflicts.

4 Given that people from Sites A and B died in different ways, do you think it is appropriate to compare the percentage of people with trauma between the two sites? Why or why not?

In the bar chart, only the percentage of individuals affected with trauma is presented. You cannot tell how many total skeletons (the total sample size) were analyzed for each site.

5 Why do you think it is important to consider sample size for each site?

6 For **Site A**, researchers examined 486 individuals, as compared to **Site C** with only ten individuals. Which site do you think is a more representative sample of the site's population?

Finally, you want to get a sense of the spatial distribution of the sites across the world. Sites have been plotted on the map below, and each black dot represents one site location.

7 Describe one pattern you observe in the distribution of sites. Consider if sites are clustered together or isolated. Are any regions over- or underrepresented? Remember you're trying to get a global overview of violence patterns.

8 Do you think you can adequately test your hypothesis given the data presented in this activity? Why or why not? If you were designing future analyses, what could you do to improve the study?

Interpretation

14. Symbo-phone

Leah McCurdy

Symbols are everywhere today and have been used by humans for a long time to communicate visually. Symbols are the foundation for writing systems; and thus, written history. The development of writing systems involved codifying a set of symbols that often stood for components of a verbal language, including both whole ideas (or words) and separate sounds (or syllables). Symbols of a writing system that represent whole ideas or words are called logograms or logographs. Those that represent syllables are called logosyllabic symbols or logosyllabic glyphs. Many early written languages, including Egyptian and Maya hieroglyphics, incorporate both logographic and logosyllabic symbols.

Epigraphy is the study of ancient writing systems. One important task of epigraphic studies is to understand how a writing system changed over time or evolved into new forms.

Have you ever played the game Telephone? That game focuses on passing on verbal information, and how it changes as new people hear the information. This activity, Symbo-phone, focuses on communicating visual information, through symbols. Changes over "generations" simulate how symbolic systems of the past, such as cuneiform or hieroglyphic writing, evolved over time as new generations learned, used, and modified them.

- **Part I:** Use the worksheet provided to design and render a communicative symbol that has a specific meaning to you. Participate in the simulation of generational knowledge transfer.

- **Part II:** Analyze the changes to the symbol you originally created.

Part I

FIRST GENERATION

Create a simple symbol that has a specific meaning. It can be logographic or logosyllabic. Draw the symbol on the left and describe its meaning on the right.

Symbol	Meaning

Teach your symbol to someone else. This person is the second generation. Pass this sheet on to him or her and teach the information visually, in written form, and verbally.

SECOND GENERATION

Based on the first generation's instruction, copy the symbol in your own hand on the left and describe its meaning in your own words on the right.

Symbol	Meaning

There has been a political takeover. The new leader is asking all artists and scribes to redesign the visual system to suit their visual preferences. Teach your symbol to another person (third generation) but instruct him or her to change one component of the symbol that will affect its appearance but not its meaning. Pass this sheet on to that person.

THIRD GENERATION

Based on the instructions from the second generation, draw the symbol with a change on the left and describe its meaning in your own words on the right.

Symbol	Meaning

Teach your symbol to another person (fourth generation). Pass this sheet on to him or her and teach the information visually, in written form, and verbally.

FOURTH GENERATION

Based on the instructions from the third generation, copy the symbol in your own hand on the left and describe its meaning in your own words on the right.

Symbol	Meaning

A famine struck your region and you were never able to teach the next generation about this symbol in person. So much time passes that all written information is lost. Conceal (but do not destroy) the written description of the meaning from *all generations*. Pass this sheet on to the fifth generation *without any verbal instruction*. They should *see only the visual record!*

FIFTH GENERATION

Much time has passed and knowledge from previous generations has been lost. Copy the symbol based on the available visual record. Attempt to reconstruct the symbol's meaning and write a description on the right.

Symbol	Meaning

There has been a fire and all visual record of the symbol is lost. Remove (but do not destroy) the visual record by concealing the drawings of all generations. Pass this sheet on to the sixth generation and share with them the written meanings that remain unconcealed.

SIXTH GENERATION

Based on the information provided by the fifth generation, draw the symbol as best you can on the left and describe its meaning in your own words on the right.

Symbol	Meaning

You are the final generation. Help this record sheet get back to its originator.

Part II

Time travel to see how your symbol evolved over time. Find your original Part I Worksheet, remove all concealment, and answer the questions below.

1 Which event created more change in the symbol's evolution: the takeover, the famine, or the fire? Describe the change and why you think that event was so impactful.

2 Imagine many more, similar, events occurred over a 1,000-year period. What other changes would you expect to impact on this symbol?

3 Imagine you are an archaeologist 2,000 years in the future. You find the sixth-generation symbol. Eventually, you also find that one of the first-generation symbols did survive. Are they similar enough to identify them as part of the same group? Why or why not?

15. Clocking Change

Crystal A. Dozier

Humans have come to occupy every landscape on the globe, starting from our evolutionary homeland in Africa. Due to our relatively short evolutionary history, humans are extremely genetically (genotypically) similar. Phenotypically (meaning the way that the genes are expressed as our appearance), humans can seem more diverse than we actually are. Geneticists and evolutionary anthropologists study the expansion of our species through genetic variability and archaeological evidence.

Genetic material can change over time, due to several mechanisms. In this activity, you will explore the concept of mutation, involving *random change* in DNA. Mutations happen randomly, but the chances of mutation are relatively stable in most contexts. By calculating the number of mutations that have occurred in the genetic code, scientists can estimate how long it has been since different populations or species diverged (meaning became so different that they could not produce viable offspring). This concept is called the molecular clock.

In this activity, you will simulate the biological diversity of modern humans as we spread across the globe. We know some of the patterns of human dispersal from archaeological remains. We evolved in, and most of our history is within, Africa. From there, we spread to the Near East and Asia. Humans did not arrive in Europe until late in the Pleistocene, commonly known as the Ice Age. Lastly, humans colonized the Americas. As these human colonizers moved, their genetics certainly mutated. However, the patterns of these mutations may not be reflected in the phenotypic diversity that is commonly used to delineate peoples today. The genetic diversity of our species is mostly held in our evolutionary homeland.

For this activity, you will need ten differently colored markers, pencils, or dot stickers:

- Each color represents a lineage of people. Different colors indicate different variations on a gene. For this activity, these variations have no effect on group survival.

- Starting 200,000 years ago in East Africa, you will establish your first human lineage with a color of your choice.

- For every 5,000 years that passes, you will start a new lineage. Every new lineage needs to be descended from a previous lineage, *thus sharing the same color on the same continent.* The steps will tell you when to introduce a new lineage to a new area. New lineages can populate only a continent that has already been colonized. *Remember: populations in previous continents keep reproducing!*

- New variations (colors) will be introduced every 20,000 years through mutation. *Remember: new variations do NOT arise only in new territories.* The rate of mutation is the same for all lineages, so new variations (colors) will most likely arise in the most populated area.

Follow the above steps to populate your map (on p. 54).

YA = "years ago"

200,000 YA	Start your first lineage in East Africa
195,000 YA	New lineage
190,000 YA	New lineage
185,000 YA	New lineage
180,000 YA	New lineage with mutation!
175,000 YA	New lineage
170,000 YA	New lineage
165,000 YA	New lineage
160,000 YA	New lineage with mutation!
155,000 YA	New lineage
150,000 YA	New lineage
145,000 YA	New lineage
140,000 YA	New lineage with mutation!
135,000 YA	New lineage
130,000 YA	New lineage
125,000 YA	New lineage
120,000 YA	New lineage with mutation!
115,000 YA	New lineage
110,000 YA	New lineage
105,000 YA	Lineage migrates into the Middle East
100,000 YA	New lineage with mutation! Mutation occurs in Africa
95,000 YA	New lineage in either Africa or the Middle East
90,000 YA	New lineage
85,000 YA	New lineage
80,000 YA	New lineage with mutation! Mutation occurs in either Africa or the Middle East
75,000 YA	New lineage
70,000 YA	New lineage
65,000 YA	Lineage migrates to Southeast Asia
60,000 YA	New lineage with mutation! Mutation occurs in either Africa or the Middle East
55,000 YA	Lineage migrates to Australia
50,000 YA	New lineage
45,000 YA	Lineage migrates to Europe
40,000 YA	New lineage with mutation!
35,000 YA	New lineage
30,000 YA	Lineage migrates to Japan
25,000 YA	New lineage
20,000 YA	New lineage with mutation!
15,000 YA	Lineage migrates to North America
10,000 YA	New lineages (without mutation) emerge in Africa, the Middle East, and Asia
5,000 YA	Lineage migrates to Oceania. New lineages (without mutation) emerge in all continents.

Reflective questions

1 Looking at your map, which continent has the most biological diversity? Which continent has the least?

2 How do archaeologists know when humans got to each continent?

3 What are the shortcomings of a "molecular clock" model for mutation?

4 How does a concept of "race" match or not match with your simulation?

5 What simplifications are in this simulation that don't reflect the reality of the past?

16. Seek and You Shall Find

Leah McCurdy

Indiana Jones paints an inaccurate picture of what archaeological research is like, for many reasons. While fieldwork and data collection (minus the whip) are essential, that is not all that an archaeologist does. Much of our work involves reading and writing reports, articles, and books so that we can be as up to date on recent findings as possible, share our own findings, and provide insights to other scholars. Like other scientists, archaeologists use theory and explanatory approaches to guide their research. Theories provide a structure for developing hypotheses, collecting and analyzing data, as well as making interpretations. Common theories and approaches in archaeology are included in the table on p. 58.

Some of these theories and approaches are considered more relevant to archaeological research today, whereas some were applied more in the past. Archaeology today involves rigorous scientific means to collect and evaluate data with the goal of answering important questions. Through appropriate theoretical applications and informed approaches, archaeologists continually add to our collective understanding of the past.

One important way that we ensure the quality of archaeological science and publications is through peer review. When an archaeologist writes an article or book, and submits it to an academic journal or publisher, other archaeologists who specialize in similar areas review it. Reviewers determine if the work is good enough to be published as an academic resource. This does not mean that they have to agree completely with the interpretations, but that they see that the study and conclusions reached are logical, ethical, and worthy of being part of the academic literature on the subject. When accepted through peer review, articles and books are considered first-tier sources that can be referenced by other scholars in future studies and publications. Resources that are not peer-reviewed are considered second-tier because they have not been rigorously studied and evaluated by other experts.

Through this activity, you will conduct a brief research project to find a first-tier academic archaeological article presenting data and interpretations using a theory or approach of your choice. Using library or online resources, you will locate an academic source using that theory as applied to a real-world archaeological example. You will read the article and assess its use of the theory or approach.

Migrationist approach	Post-processual approach
Diffusion theory	Structuralist approach (post-processual)
Processual approach	Critical theory (post-processual)
Marxist theory (processual)	Neo-marxist theory (post-processual)
Evolutionary perspective (processual)	Agency/Practice theory
Cognitive archaeology	Material engagement approach

1 Choose a theory or approach from the table in the activity description that interests you:

Theory or approach: _____

In the space below, write two to three sentences outlining the most significant aspects or goals of this theory or approach.

2 Determine the best place or means available to you to find an academic article that applies this theory or approach to archaeological data. These are some possibilities and strategies:

a Use the general and/or database search functions available through your campus library's website.

b Use the book catalog search available at your on-campus library.

c Use online academic search engines, such as JSTOR or Google Scholar.

3 Search for *a first-tier article* employing the theory or approach you chose above. Use these strategies to get started:

a Depending on the theory or approach, you may need to tailor your search to articles from particular periods in the history of archaeology. For example, diffusion theory is older than the material-engagement approach.

b Try searching by author. Which scholars are most associated with particular theories or approaches; and therefore, are most likely to write about them?

c Are there any journals that are completely devoted to your theory or approach? Many archaeological journals specialize in publishing articles that focus on specific approaches. You are much more likely to find relevant articles by finding a specialized journal.

4 Collect several article options. Read the abstracts (a short summary provided on the first page or under the title) to determine which article meets your needs:

a Does it incorporate and apply your theory/approach?

b Does it present and discuss an archaeological dataset? Does it describe evidence and findings?

5 Once you have made your final selection, read the article in full. Taking notes in the margins, underlining, and highlighting key sections is highly recommended. Based on your reading of the article, complete tasks **a** to **d**:

a Create a bibliographic reference for the article in a citation style with which you are familiar. You will need to record the author name(s), the date of publication, the article title, the name of the journal in which the article was published, the volume number, the issue number, and the page numbers.

b Describe the background. Where is it located? What time period is being studied? What type of archaeological remains or material culture is the author focused on?

c Describe the study. What is the overall goal? What is the data/dataset that is being analyzed? How did the author collect that data? What type of analysis did he or she conduct?

d Describe how the theory or approach is applied. What are the primary interpretations or conclusions? How do these interpretations relate to the theory or approach? Do they support the approach? Do they disprove the approach?

Archaeology and the Public

17. The Pulse on the Past
Joshua J. Lynch

Few fields can capture the attention and imagination of the public like archaeology. Engaging with prehistory (and history) often sparks strong emotional and intellectual reactions from adults and children alike. Despite the power of archaeology to inspire, reaching out to the public and making archaeological research accessible to the masses is an often-neglected component of the discipline. Many archaeologists consider encouraging stewardship of archaeological resources by the general public to be a key responsibility of professionals in the field and essential for the future of archaeology.

In this activity, you will interview a friend or family member about his or her exposure to archaeology. A list of questions designed to guide your interview is provided (on p. 63). These questions should provide a framework for assessing the interviewee's understanding of archaeology as a field, his or her exposure to archaeological research, the connection he or she feels to this research, and the level of interest he or she has in the archaeology all around. This is an opportunity to conduct a formal and ethical interview from an anthropological and/or sociological point of view.

Select a friend or family member to interview. Other students cannot be interviewees.

Review the questions provided and generate at least two additional questions of interest to you. You can also generate questions that come to mind during the interview.

Conduct the interview:

- Provide the interviewee with the consent form (including copies of the questions).

- Do not begin the interview before you have consent (the signed document).

- Transcribe all responses by taking detailed notes.

- Consider using recording technology (i.e. a smartphone or laptop) to document the interview. If you choose to record your interview, be sure that you obtain explicit permission from the interviewee.

CONSENT FORM

I, _____ (student name), am conducting an interview about the public perception of archaeology as a large collaborative class study. I am seeking your consent to interview you for this purpose.

CONSENT FOR PARTICIPATION IN INTERVIEW RESEARCH:

1 I understand that the project is designed to gather information for academic purposes.
2 My participation in this project is voluntary. I understand that I will not be paid for my participation. I may withdraw and discontinue participation at any time. I have the right to decline to answer any question.
3 I understand that the interviewer will not identify me by name in any reports using information obtained from this interview.
4 I have read and understand the information above. I have had all my questions answered to my satisfaction. I voluntarily agree to participate in this study.

Signature of participant _____

Date _____

Interview questions

1 What does the word "archaeology" make you think of?

2 Did/Do you spend much time in school discussing archaeology or examining history using evidence from archaeological research?

3 Where do you get most of your information about modern archaeology? Museums, books, magazines, articles, blogs, television, the Internet?

4 Can you give me some examples of archaeological discoveries that have been made in your lifetime?

5 Have you ever visited a museum that featured archaeological exhibits? If so, what part of the exhibit had the most impact on you?

6 Have you ever found any artifacts? Do you think that citizens should be allowed to own artifacts or archaeological sites? What would you do if you found an artifact?

7 In the past year, have you seen any news related to archaeology on social media platforms? (Facebook, Twitter, Instagram, etc.)

8 Can you think of any examples of archaeology (prehistoric or historic) in your local community? Would you be interested in seeing more displays, exhibits, and informative signage related to local archaeology?

9 What role do you think that archaeology has in the world today?

10 STUDENT-GENERATED QUESTION # 1:

11 STUDENT-GENERATED QUESTION # 2:

As a reaction to your interview, write a short paper including the following.
To prepare your paper, respond in three to five sentences to each segment below.

1 What was the interview process like? How would you do it differently?
Were you able to use any examples from this course to facilitate discussion
with your interviewee?

2 Did any of the answers you received surprise you? Did any part of the interview
effect how you feel about the public's relationship with archaeology?

3 Based on the information you gathered in the interview, and your own experience,
can you think of any ways to improve archaeologists' efforts to disseminate
information to the public?

Heritage

18. Curate It!

Elanor Sonderman, Jordan Pratt, and Heather Thakar

Heritage management involves the preservation and maintenance of sites, objects, and ideas (intangible heritage) that have cultural and/or historical significance. Managing shared cultural heritage is an integral part of preserving the excavated archaeological record in perpetuity. Heritage management includes accounting for the long-term preservation of the physical integrity of individual objects, as well as ensuring the preservation of their cultural context through engagement with descendant communities and other stakeholders.

In this activity, you will explore the processes involved in cultural heritage management. The steps taken here will help you understand the many facets of heritage management and how archaeologists, curators, and collections managers work with objects and communities to protect our collective past.

Observe an archaeological or anthropological collection. Options include a collection held at your college or university, a local museum, or digital materials.

Project/site name: _____

Site no. or ID: _____

Excavation/collection date: _____

Excavated/collected by: _____

Site location: _____

Provenience: _____

Number of objects: _____ Relative age _____
(pre-historic/historic)

1 Complete the site tag above, filling in all pertinent information about your collection.

2 Observe one object in the collection in detail and record the following information:

   a Object type or description: what is the object? If you do not know the object type, describe what it looks like.

b Material class(es): what is the object made of? (E.g. stone, metal, ceramic, glass, bone, basketry, textiles, leather). List all applicable materials.

c Object condition: Is the object complete or incomplete? Is the object worn? If yes, describe how (e.g. chipped, bleached, oxidized, etc.). Is the object brittle?

3 Research and identify the preservation issues and ideal curation standards for caring for the object you selected in Question 2. Consult your textbook and the *National Park Service Museum Handbook* Part I, Chapter 8 and/or Part I, Appendix I for guidance (www.nps.gov/museum).

4 Research and identify potential cultural issues or concerns based on the object's likely cultural affiliation. Questions to keep in mind:

a Does NAGPRA (Native American Graves Protection and Repatriation Act) apply to your object?

b Who (researchers, educators, descendant communities, landowners, etc.) might be interested in your object?

c How might these groups be affected by research, conservation treatments, and preservation of your object?

5 Create a curation plan (based on what you discovered in Questions 3 and 4) by addressing the following:

a Does the object need conservation? (Yes/No). If so, which method? Provide a justification.

b Does the object need to be placed in new packaging? (Yes/No). If so, what type of packaging or storage furniture is recommended?

c What environmental conditions should the artifact be stored in?

d What accommodations are necessary to ensure that the concerns of all impacted groups are addressed?

19. Giving Back?

Leah McCurdy

What happens to all the artifacts that are recovered from survey and excavation? Today, governments of the countries where artifacts are found decide what happens to them. Often, artifacts of great significance are conserved and placed in the country's national or local museums.

In the past, when Western countries were colonizing other regions of the world, they were undertaking investigatory expeditions and/or excavations. It is difficult to use the term excavation, as we scientifically define it today, when discussing some of the earliest examples of "colonial archaeology." Those colonially associated investigations and archaeological projects either claimed artifacts for their home country or were meant to uphold agreements with host countries or local cultures to determine which artifacts would remain in-country and which artifacts would be claimed for the colonial power. Sometimes, archaeologists did not adhere to these agreements.

One famous example of such issues in archaeological ethics relates to the Bust of Nefertiti. This artifact of immense significance was essentially smuggled out of Egypt by archaeologists, ended up in the possession of the German government, hidden by the Nazis during World War II, and is now the centerpiece of a museum in Berlin. Egypt wants it back.

Egypt is calling for repatriation, or the return of the artifact to its country of origin. Its claim against Germany is in dispute. There are other famous examples of repatriation controversies, some of which have been resolved but many remain unresolved. In this activity, you will investigate a case of contested repatriation and take part in a debate on the topic.

Repatriation is an important topic within archaeology and international affairs today. There are no easy answers to questions of who owns what and whether objects should be repatriated. It is your task to investigate a claim from both sides. Then, argue the case for the "side" of the debate to which you are assigned.

1 Use the table below to choose which case of contested repatriation you will investigate and which "side" you will argue: FOR repatriation or AGAINST repatriation.

Last name A–D	Bust of Nefertiti FOR	Last name M–P	Bust of Nefertiti AGAINST
Last name E–G	Kennewick Man FOR	Last name Q–T	Kennewick Man AGAINST
Last name H–L	Elgin Marbles FOR	Last name U–Z	Elgin Marbles AGAINST

2 Investigate your case *from both sides of the argument*. This will ensure that you have the full context of the issue. Use this bibliography to locate reliable online forums about each case:

Desplat, Juliette. 2016. "The Nefertiti affair: the history of a repatriation debate." *The National Archives Blog*. Accessed December 26, 2017.

Elginism Staff. 2009. "Arguments for & against the return of the Elgin Marbles." *Elginism*. Accessed December 26, 2017.

Hirst, K. Kris. n.d. "What is the Kennewick Man Controversy About?" Accessed December 26, 2017.

Morelle, Rebecca. "DNA reignites Kennewick Man debate." *BBC News* (June 18, 2015).

Reuters Staff. "German foundation refuses to return Nefertiti Bust." Reuters (January 24, 2011).

Riley, Kate. 2006. "Who owns the past?" *The Seattle Times*.

Sánchez, Juan Pablo. "How the Parthenon Lost Its Marbles." *National Geographic History* (March/April 2017).

Sinclair, A. G. M. n.d. "The Kennewick Man Skeleton: Problems in the Repatriation of Ancient Skeletal Remains." *Archaeology and Contemporary Society: Ethical and Political Issues Module.* Accessed December 26, 2017.

Ward, Victoria. "Why are the Elgin marbles so controversial – and everything else you need to know." *The Telegraph* (December 5, 2014).

3 Document the Who? What? When? Where? Why? facts of the case.
Make notes that you can bring to the debate to help as you make your points.

4 Document *two primary points* that will make a strong case for your side of the argument.

a Primary Point 1:

b Primary Point 2:

5 After the debate, write a short reaction with the purpose of describing your opinion about the contested repatriation you investigated. Make sure you clearly answer this question: should the object(s) be repatriated?